UNOFFICIAL
GUIDES
JUNIOR

Starter Guide to Super Mario Party

by Josh Gregory

Cherry Lake Press
Ann Arbor, Michigan

Published in the United States of America by Cherry Lake Publishing
Ann Arbor, Michigan
www.cherrylakepublishing.com

Reading Adviser: Beth Walker Gambro, MS, Ed., Reading Consultant, Yorkville, IL

Photo Credits: Images by Josh Gregory

Cherry Lake Press is an imprint of Cherry Lake Publishing Group.

Library of Congress Cataloging-in-Publication Data has been filed and is available at catalog.loc.gov

Printed in the United States of America by
Corporate Graphics

Note from the Publisher: Websites change regularly, and their future contents are outside of our control. Supervise children when conducting any recommended online searches for extended learning opportunities.

Contents

Let's Party!

Nintendo, the creator of *Mario Party*, started in 1889. At first, they made card games and toys!

People love board games. So why not combine a board game and a video game? In 1998, Nintendo did just that. They released *Mario Party*. It was a video game unlike any other. *Mario Party* was based on a **traditional** board game. But it also had extra fun features. And it included *Super Mario* characters! These things made the game a hit.

Game Basics

Always try to get as many stars as you can playing *Mario Party*!

Up to four people can play *Mario Party*. Or you can play against the computer. Either way, you'll have fun **competing**. Roll the **virtual** dice and move across the board. Try to collect as many stars as possible. The object is simple. The player with the most stars wins!

Minigames

Win as many minigames as you can!

A big part of *Mario Party* is minigames. These smaller games pop up in the game. There are many types of minigames. They range from mazes to memory contests. Some pit players against each other. Others are team efforts. Each minigame takes a couple of minutes or less. Try your best! Winning them will lead to success in the game.

Game Controller Skills

Minigames challenge players to use their game controllers in special ways. For example, to climb a pole, players must use buttons *and* motion controls.

Which **Series?**

In *Super Mario Party*, each player uses a single Joy-Con controller.

There are many games in the *Mario Party* series. In 2018, *Super Mario Party* was released for the Nintendo Switch. Beginner players love this game. It's easy to learn. But with many new board games and minigames, it's still challenging. And it takes time to master.

Enjoyed by All

Millions of people enjoy *Mario Party*. You can play it with friends or family. It's like a board game, only better!

Starting Out

Random Choice
SL All Minigames SR
Rumble Fishing
Favorites Details Back

Minigames **mode** lets you play without starting a full game.

When you first play *Super Mario Party*, you'll start in the Party Plaza. This is the main menu of the game. Here, you can choose the number of players. You can also pick a game mode. To do this, move your character to one of the big video screens. Press the A button to select one. The most basic is Mario Party mode.

Minigames Mode

Do you just want to play minigames? Try Minigames mode. Here, you can practice the minigames you love.

Other **Modes**

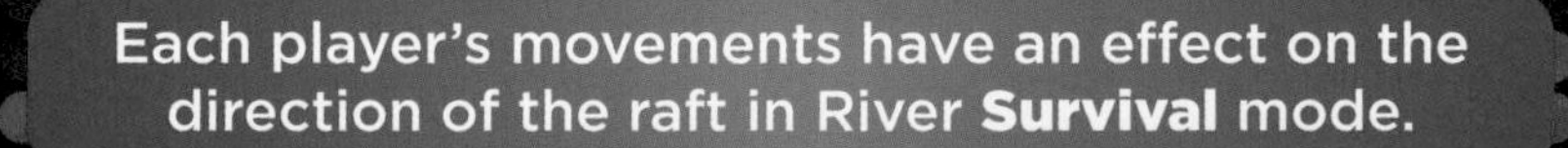

Each player's movements have an effect on the direction of the raft in River **Survival** mode.

You can also play Partner Party and River Survival modes. In Partner Party, you'll play in two teams of two players each. River Survival involves a raft. Players hold their controllers like oars. Then they move them to paddle down a river. They need to finish the course before the timer runs out!

Sound Stage

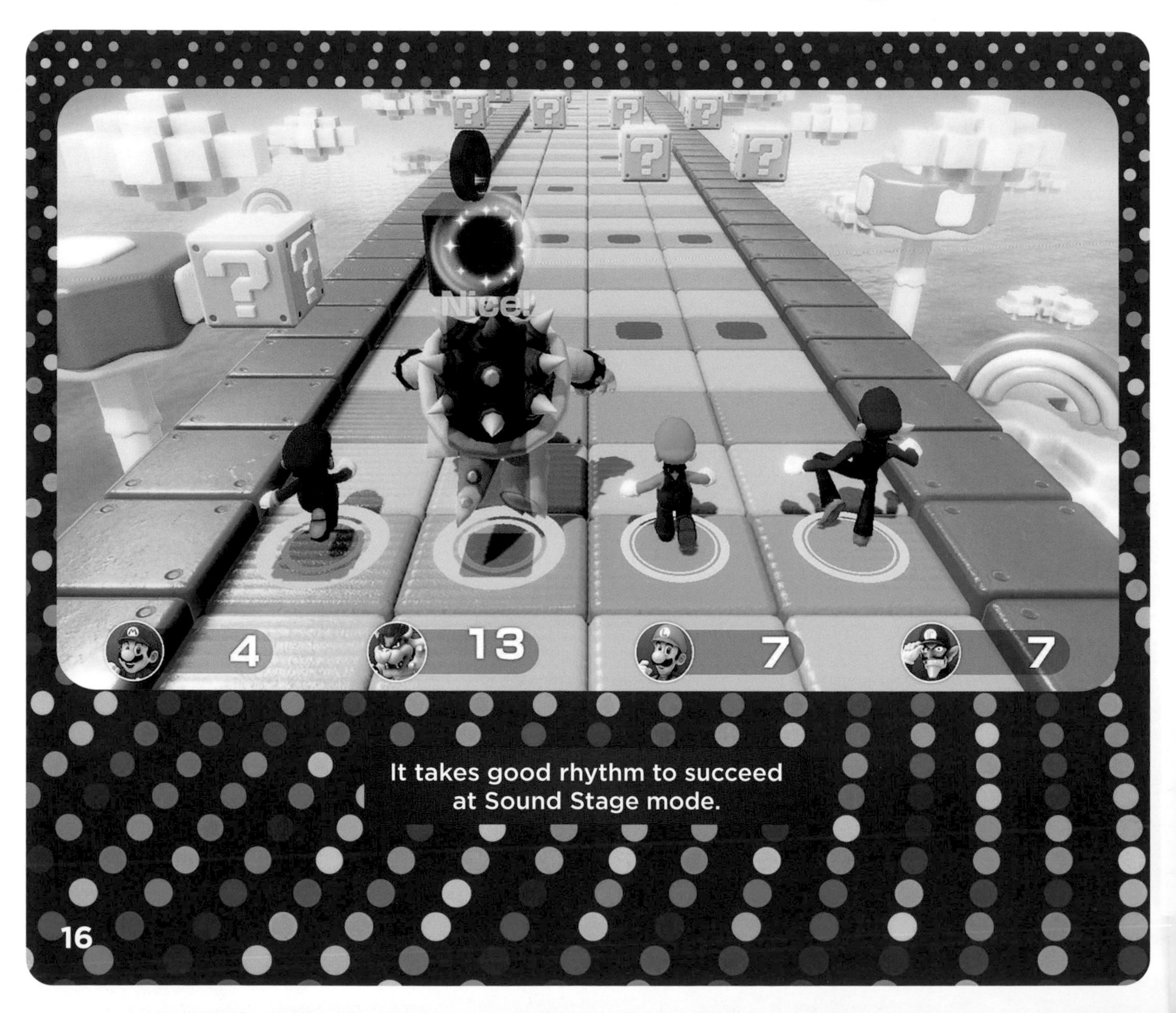

It takes good rhythm to succeed at Sound Stage mode.

Sound Stage is a musical mode. Players compete while listening to music! All the while, they move and shake their controllers. Moving your controller just right will earn you coins. The player with the most coins is the winner.

Using Coins

You can use coins to buy things at a shop. Or you can trade them for stars. Try to collect as many as you can.

Pick a Board

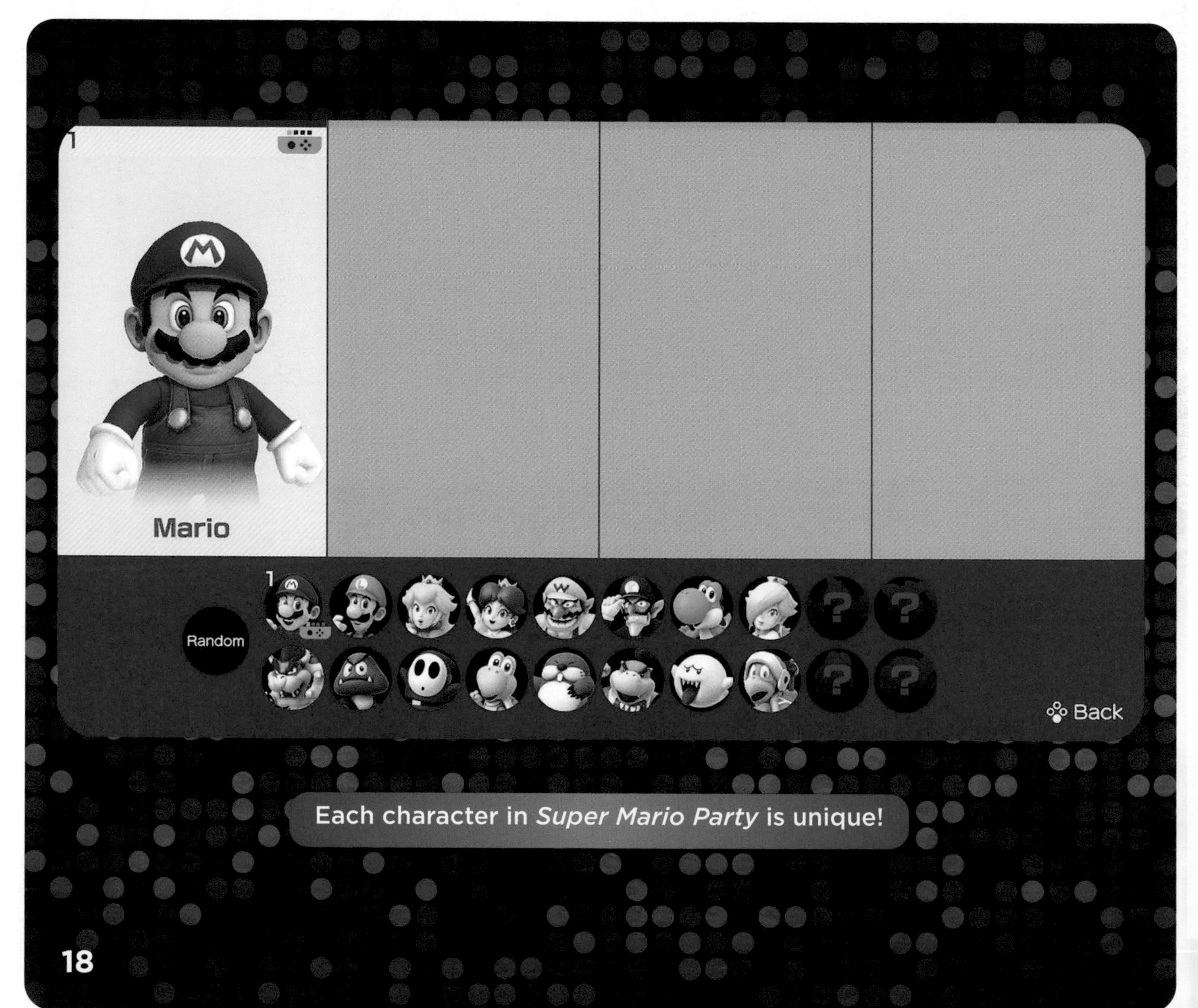
1
Mario
1
Random
Back
Each character in *Super Mario Party* is unique!

The main board game mode draws the most players. There are three boards to choose from. Each one has a different **theme**. You can also decide how long your game will last. Then each player rolls the dice. You can pick the normal dice. Or you can play special dice for more adventure!

What's Next?

Mario suggested having a party to
decide, a time-honored tradition.
SL/SR Skip

As Mario says, it's always a good idea to have a party with friends!

As you play, try to find the most stars. You won't win every game you play. But it's not always about winning. *Super Mario Party* is about having a good time. Invite your friends and family to play. Roll the dice. See where the game takes you!

Mario Party Superstars

In 2021, Nintendo released *Mario Party Superstars*. It has more than 100 minigames!

GLOSSARY

competing (kuhm-PEET-ing) playing against others in order to win

mode (MOHD) a way of operating or using a system

survival (sur-VYE-vuhl) the act of staying alive

theme (THEEM) the topic of something

traditional (truh-DISH-uh-nuhl) long-established

virtual (VUR-choo-ul) created by a computer

FIND OUT MORE

BOOKS

Gregory, Josh. *Super Mario Party: Beginner's Guide*. Ann Arbor, MI: Cherry Lake Publishing, 2022.

Loh-Hagan, Virginia. *Video Games*. Ann Arbor, MI: Cherry Lake Publishing, 2021.

Powell, Marie. *Asking Questions About Video Games*. Ann Arbor, MI: Cherry Lake Publishing, 2016.

WEBSITES

With an adult, learn more online with these suggested searches:

Mario Party Superstars for Nintendo Switch
Check out the latest updates on the upcoming sequel to *Super Mario Party*.

Super Mario Party for Nintendo Switch
Watch some videos and learn more about the different features of *Super Mario Party*.

INDEX

ABOUT THE AUTHOR

Josh Gregory is the author of more than 200 books for kids. He has written about everything from animals to technology to history. A graduate of the University of Missouri–Columbia, he currently lives in Chicago, Illinois.